MILITARY OPERATIONS
AGAINST TERRORIST GROUPS ABROAD

Implications for the United States Air Force

David Ochmanek

Prepared for the
United States Air Force

Approved for Public Release; Distribution Unlimited

RAND
Project AIR FORCE

The research reported here was sponsored by the United States Air Force under Contract F49642-01-C-0003. Further information may be obtained from the Strategic Planning Division, Directorate of Plans, Hq USAF.

Library of Congress Cataloging-in-Publication Data

Ochmanek, David A.
    Military operations against terrorist groups abroad : implications for the United States Air Force / David Ochmanek.
        p. cm.
    "MR-1738."
    Includes bibliographical references.
    ISBN 0-8330-3437-5 (pbk.)
    1. United States. Air Force—Foreign service. 2. Terrorism—Prevention. 3. War on Terrorism, 2001– I.Title.

UG633.O26 2003
358.4'00973—dc22

                                                                                      2003014992

U.S. Air Force cover photo courtesy of the DoD Joint Combat Camera Center(DoD JCCC) at www.dodimagery.afis.osd.mil. Photographer: Staff Sgt. Jeremy T. Lock.

RAND is a nonprofit institution that helps improve policy and decisionmaking through research and analysis. RAND® is a registered trademark. RAND's publications do not necessarily reflect the opinions or policies of its research sponsors.

Cover design by Stephen Bloodsworth

Published 2003 by RAND
1700 Main Street, P.O. Box 2138, Santa Monica, CA 90407-2138
1200 South Hayes Street, Arlington, VA 22202-5050
201 North Craig Street, Suite 202, Pittsburgh, PA 15213-1516
RAND URL: http://www.rand.org/
To order RAND documents or to obtain additional information, contact Distribution Services: Telephone: (310) 451-7002; Fax: (310) 451-6915; Email: order@rand.org

The threat posed by international terrorists to Americans and their way of life has placed new demands on the national security apparatus of the United States. Within weeks of the attacks of September 11, 2001, U.S. military forces were engaged in intensive efforts to dismantle al Qaeda and related groups, apprehend or kill their members, and destroy their sanctuaries. Those operations have continued, albeit at varying degrees of scope and intensity, not only in Afghanistan and its neighboring states, but also in such places as the Philippines, Yemen, and the Republic of Georgia. From the standpoint of defense planners, it is not accurate to say that the attacks of September 11 "changed everything": all of the missions and responsibilities that had been levied on the U.S. armed forces prior to the attacks remain. But important new requirements have been added and these will almost certainly endure for many years to come. The purpose of this study is to help defense planners anticipate the types of demands that future operations against terrorists will place on the armed forces of the United States— particularly the United States Air Force. The discussion here focuses on the main determinant of those demands—efforts to disrupt or destroy terrorist groups by attacking them abroad.

Force planning and resource allocation must be based on projections of the nature, scope, pace, and frequency of future operations. Accordingly, strategy, which prescribes the ways in which the nation's resources are to be harnessed to the pursuit of its objectives, is the first step in the force planning process. Defense planners must be cognizant not only of the broad missions assigned to their forces but also of the ways in which those forces would likely be employed to accomplish those missions. For many years, U.S. planners and operational commanders alike have worked from a shared picture of the basic concepts and strategies that would govern the operations of forces in major theater conflicts. This study provides an analogous "generic" strategy for U.S. military operations against terrorist groups overseas. In addition to spelling out the key components of that strategy, it offers ideas about the types of capabilities that air forces will likely be called upon to provide in executing it.

Shortly after the September 11 attacks, Air Force Chief of Staff General John Jumper asked RAND to conduct a study entitled "Thinking Strategically About Combating Terrorism." This year-long project was divided into four research tasks, each tackling different but complementary aspects of the counterterrorism problem:

- Threat assessment: identifying the character and boundaries of the threat

- The international dimension: assessing the impact of coalition and other international actors on U.S. options

- Strategy: designing an overarching counterterror strategy

- Implications for the Air Force: identifying promising applications of air- and space power.

This report presents a summary of the findings from the fourth task.

Initial work on the research outlined here took place in both the Strategy and Doctrine program and the Aerospace Force Development program. Ultimately, the study was completed in the Strategy and Doctrine program. Comments are welcome and may be directed to the author; to Tim Bonds, director of Project AIR FORCE's (PAF's) Aerospace Force Development program; or to Ted Harshberger, director of PAF's Strategy and Doctrine program. Research for this report was completed in early 2003.

A related publication is:

- Nora Bensahel, *The Counterterrorism Coalitions: Cooperation with Europe, NATO, and the European Union*, MR-1746-AF.

PROJECT AIR FORCE

Project AIR FORCE (PAF), a division of RAND, is the Air Force's federally funded research and development center for studies and analyses. PAF provides the Air Force with independent analyses of policy alternatives affecting the deployment, employment, combat readiness, and support of current and future aerospace forces. Research is conducted in four programs: Aerospace Force Development; Manpower, Readiness, and Training; Resource Management; and Strategy and Doctrine.

Additional information about PAF is available on our web site at http://www.rand.org/paf.

CONTENTS

Figures

Tables

Although the armed forces of the United States do not bear the sole or even the primary responsibility for protecting the nation against terrorist attacks, they do play important roles in this regard and these roles are, in some cases, placing new demands on the armed forces. Nowhere is this more true than in cases in which a foreign government shares our interest in eradicating terrorism but lacks the wherewithal to do so effectively on its own. Such states—call them "willing but weak"—span a wide gamut, from traditional security partners, such as the Philippines, to states with which the United States lacks a long history of security cooperation, such as Yemen. Some, like the governments of Uzbekistan and the Philippines, seek to prosecute fairly aggressive operations against terrorist groups on their territory. Others, such as Sudan, Indonesia, and Somalia, may have a more ambivalent attitude or simply be incapable of mounting effective operations. Given this wide range of potential operating environments, one would expect a wide variance in the types of operations that U.S. forces might be called upon to conduct in these countries. Is it possible to generalize about the demands of counterterrorist operations?

The mission of U.S. forces in these countries is clear: to eliminate or neutralize terrorist groups threatening U.S. interests. Operations in support of this mission will generally be undertaken in cooperation with (and, indeed, in support of) forces of the host country. Specific campaigns will generally comprise combinations of the following operational objectives (see pages 5–20):

- Strengthen the capabilities and will of host government forces
- Disrupt the activities of terrorists
- Help to alienate terrorists from the populace
- Gather intelligence about terrorist networks and activities around the world
- Protect friendly forces and bases
- Find and capture or kill terrorists
- Prevent terrorists from acquiring, retaining, or using chemical, biological, radiological, or nuclear (CBRN) weapons.

If this vision of future U.S. military operations against terrorist groups is an accurate guide to strategy, it suggests that the widely used term "war on terrorism" is unfortunate. The sorts of operations envisaged here are likely to be long-term efforts in which the use of force, at least by U.S. military personnel, is only sporadic. Indeed, military operations against terrorist groups often will have to have much in common with effective counterinsurgency operations if they are to be successful. Accordingly, the hallmarks of effective counterterrorist efforts in these "willing but weak" states generally will be:

- The host government and not the United States plays the leading role in hunting down the terrorists
- The terrorists are subjected to relentless pressure and are not able to determine the tempo and timing of operations but rather are forced to react to government-initiated operations
- Operations are information intensive, depending crucially on accurate information on the activities, location, and identities of the terrorists
- Most important, the government must win the support of the populace, alienating the terrorists from potential sources of support (see pages 9–14).

These considerations point to a demanding set of operating environments for U.S. forces charged with countering terrorist groups

abroad. Those forces will be called upon to forge strong relationships with host-country personnel, to show great discretion in their
conduct of operations, and to maintain a low profile in the host
country yet be able to react swiftly and effectively when promising
targets arise.

The United States Air Force will be called upon to provide many important capabilities, assets, and skill sets to counterterrorist operations abroad. Chief among these are:

- Surveillance platforms, operators, and analysts
- Language-qualified personnel—commissioned officers as well as
  enlisted—to help train and advise host-country forces, interact
  with others in-country, and analyze the intelligence "take" from
  human and communications intelligence (HUMINT and
  COMINT) sources
- Security police and other force-protection assets
- Base operating support personnel and equipment to provide vital functions, such as communications, housing, and transportation at a wide range of operating locations
- Combat search and rescue (for U.S. and host-country personnel)
  as well as special operations forces (SOF) insertion and extraction capabilities
- Humanitarian relief assets, including engineers, doctors and
  dentists, public health specialists, tactical airlift aircraft, and
  crews (see pages 32–34).

ACKNOWLEDGMENTS

The author wishes to thank a number of RAND colleagues who contributed to the research behind this report and to its completion. First and foremost, Stephen Hosmer provided invaluable guidance throughout. A lifelong expert on insurgency and counterinsurgency, Steve freely shared insights about the parallels between insurgent and terrorist groups and about the relevance of counterinsurgency strategy to the fight against terrorists. Ted Harshberger and David Shlapak reviewed successive drafts of the report, prodding the author to clarify, refine, and expand upon a number of points. David Orletsky, Sara Daly, and Major Mike Pietrucha (AF/XOXS) provided thoughtful and constructive peer reviews of the final draft. Their comments enhanced the organization, accuracy, and clarity of the report. Miriam Schafer attended to the preparation of graphics and the formatting of the overall document, and Jeanne Heller patiently and expertly edited the final text.

Chapter One

INTRODUCTION

If the horrific attacks of September 11, 2001, did nothing else, they provided a stunning demonstration of America's vulnerability to attacks by small numbers of determined fanatics. The root causes of such fanaticism can be debated endlessly, but one thing seems clear: Modern technology and its dispersion are placing increasingly destructive instruments at the disposal of growing numbers of people. As long as groups exist that see it as in their interest to use violence against Americans and American interests, the threat of terrorist attacks that are able to inflict hundreds or thousands of casualties will loom over our society.

Providing security in this environment will require sustained and far-reaching national efforts encompassing intelligence gathering and assessment, law enforcement, military operations, border controls, public health and safety, and many other instruments of national policy and power. This campaign to counter terrorist groups will entail defensive as well as offensive measures; it will extend overseas as well as throughout our own nation, involving many other governments in cooperative efforts; it will involve officials at the federal, state, and local levels; and it will affect the private and public sectors. The mix of instruments applied to any particular group or situation will vary according to the threat posed and its context.

The purpose of this study is to help planners in the defense community to better understand the sorts of demands that this national counterterrorist effort might place on U.S. military forces and capabilities. The report focuses on the types of operations that U.S. military forces will likely be called upon to conduct overseas toward eliminating or weakening terrorist groups—a key element of the "offensive" portion of the national counterterrorist strategy. Those operations will be shaped, in the first instance, by the political setting in which targeted groups are operating.

The inhabited portions of the earth's landmass are demarcated, at least nominally, into states. Figure 1 provides a means for sorting among states according to two criteria: the degree to which each state opposes the existence and operations of a particular terrorist group, and the degree to which each state is capable of countering that group within its own borders. The resulting categorization highlights the differences in strategy that the United States and its armed forces will use in countering terrorist threats.

States lying in the upper left-hand quadrant of Figure 1 strongly oppose the terrorist group (in this case, al Qaeda) and have at their disposal fairly effective mechanisms for countering it, at least within

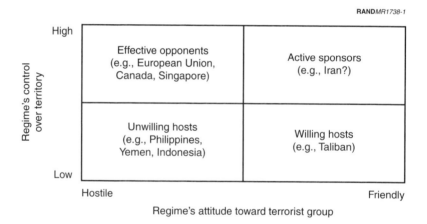

Figure 1—U.S. Strategy and Operations Are Shaped by the Nature of the Regime and the Threat

their own borders.[1] U.S. military forces will generally play at most minor roles in countering terrorism within these states. The governments of these states have police and internal security forces that are quite capable of dealing with terrorist cells in their countries, once those cells have been identified and located. Accordingly, the most valuable resource that the United States government can provide to these governments (and receive from them) is intelligence and investigative information relative to terrorist operations. Military assistance will generally be limited to combined training and exchanges between specialized counterterrorist units.

The upper right-hand quadrant includes states that are deemed capable of controlling the activities of terrorist groups within their borders but that are suspected of assisting or at least tolerating the presence of elements of a particular group. Today, no regime dares to harbor or support al Qaeda operatives openly, although Iran (like Iraq under Saddam Hussein's regime) has been accused publicly of allowing prominent al Qaeda members to dwell within its borders, at least temporarily. If firm evidence were available of such a relationship, numerous instruments of national power could be brought to bear in an attempt to compel the targeted regime to change its policies. Military force could be one of these instruments. Threats or actual attacks against assets valued by the regime could be used to attempt to coerce enemy leaders into changing their policies. U.S. forces might also be called upon to destroy infrastructure used by terrorist groups in such countries or to capture or kill through overt or covert means, terrorists operating there. Failing that, military forces could be used to attempt to bring down the offending regime, if necessary through a combined-arms invasion. As important as such operations would be in these cases, they would not impose qualitatively new demands on U.S. military forces: attacking the infrastructures of enemy nations and defeating their fielded forces is what U.S. military forces have long prepared to do as one of their primary missions.

---

[1]Evaluations of each state's counterterror competence are subjective and, of course, relative. Even the most competent of governments will find it nearly impossible to identify, locate, monitor, and, if appropriate, detain all of the terrorists, potential terrorists, and their supporters within its jurisdiction.

The lower right-hand quadrant of the figure is essentially empty today. It would be occupied by states in which a terrorist group was operating and where the government lacked the capability to evict it but refused to cooperate with U.S. antiterrorism efforts. Sudan fell into this category in the mid-1990s, as did Afghanistan under Taliban rule. To the extent that Somalia can be said to have a functioning government, it might be argued that it falls into this category today. The Taliban's refusal to turn over al Qaeda's leadership after September 11 led it to suffer a predictable fate: forcible regime change via a U.S.-led military intervention.

Finally, the lower left-hand quadrant of the figure is, from the standpoint of defense planners, the most interesting set of cases. (It is also probably the most populous.) Included here are states that, to one degree or another, have declared their willingness to cooperate with the United States in suppressing the activities of a terrorist group but that lack the capacity to do so effectively. This category encompasses a wide range of potential partner states. They include traditional allies, such as the Philippines; governments that are energetically combating terrorists but that have checkered human-rights records (Uzbekistan); governments with more ambivalent attitudes toward terrorist operations (Indonesia, Yemen); and failed states unable to impose order in their societies (Somalia). The bulk of the remainder of this study addresses issues of strategy, operations, and military capabilities relevant to states in this quadrant.

Chapter Two posits and elaborates on the major components of a "generic" operational strategy for fighting terrorist groups in countries that need outside assistance. Chapter Three considers some of the shortcomings in U.S. forces' capabilities to locate, identify, and attack terrorist groups and related targets, pointing to emerging technologies and techniques that might help to address those shortfalls. Finally, Chapter Four considers the long-term demands of a new "steady state" security environment in which U.S. military forces are engaged in sustained efforts to suppress terrorist groups abroad.

Chapter Two

A "GENERIC" OPERATIONAL STRATEGY: A TEMPLATE FOR PLANNING

Military operations against terrorist groups abroad will be shaped by the circumstances peculiar to each country and situation. Host-country governments will place different sorts of constraints on the deployment and operations of U.S. forces on their territory, and the capabilities of their own forces will vary. Likewise, terrorist groups pose different types of threats, depending on their strength (both locally and beyond their home regions) and the level of external support they might enjoy. And, as with any military operation, the terrain, weather, transportation infrastructure, and other features of the environment must be taken into account when planning and conducting operations.

That said, planners need some sort of conceptual model or template of prospective operations to prepare forces and develop capabilities. Toward this end, it is necessary to define the principal elements of a "generic" operational strategy designed to weaken or eliminate terrorist groups operating abroad. Combatant commanders charged with devising and implementing such operations will generally pursue some or all of the following operational objectives:

- Strengthen the capabilities and will of host-government forces

- Disrupt the activities of terrorists

- Help to alienate terrorists from the populace

- Gather intelligence about terrorist networks and activities around the world

- Protect friendly forces and bases
- Find and capture or kill terrorists
- Prevent terrorists from acquiring, retaining, or using chemical, biological, radiological, or nuclear (CBRN) weapons.

Together, the choice of objectives, the means for pursuing them, and the weight of effort applied to them over time define the overall campaign plan in any given country or region.[1] The remainder of this study spells out what each of these objectives might entail in future military operations against terrorist groups and, collectively, what such operations might imply for the United States Air Force and the Department of Defense more broadly.

The strategy developed here proceeds from the central hypothesis that terrorist groups seeking to operate in countries opposed to their presence exhibit many of the same characteristics as insurgent groups. For example, like insurgents, terrorists must operate in ways that make it difficult for governments to identify them, yet they require some measure of support (or at least tolerance) from elements of the populace. These requirements prompt such groups to conduct operations designed to avoid direct confrontation with numerically superior forces. And terrorism, like insurgency, is at root a political phenomenon. Its perpetrators often seek to undermine the legitimacy of opposing governments, through both ideological means and the use of violence. For these reasons, operational strategy against terrorist groups ought to have much in common with counterinsurgency strategies.

STRENGTHEN THE CAPABILITIES AND WILL OF HOST-COUNTRY FORCES

One of the most important roles that U.S. forces can play in the fight against terrorist groups is to train, advise, and assist the forces of other nations in counterinsurgency and counterterrorist operations.

---

[1]The practice of disaggregating operational strategy into its constituent objectives and tasks was developed by Glenn A. Kent. For a primer on this method, see David Thaler, *Strategies to Tasks: A Framework for Linking Means and Ends*, RAND, MR-300-AF, 1993.

The forces of many battleground countries today lack the tools, the training, and, in some cases, the motivation to conduct effective operations against terrorist groups that are often elusive, well armed, and highly committed to their cause. With time and sustained effort, U.S. military training missions can make a real difference.[2]

Training for ground combat forces typically focuses on individual skills, such as weapons training and marksmanship, and on small-unit tactics, such as patrolling, ambush, and assault. Air force and navy personnel may receive training as well, as may specialists in important support functions such as intelligence, communications, engineering, and logistics.

U.S. military personnel engaged in training the forces of other countries can greatly facilitate the adoption of new weapons and other systems by host-country forces by providing hands-on assistance in the operation and maintenance of the new systems, as well as helping host-country forces gain proficiency in the tactics and techniques appropriate for employing these systems. Thus, there are great synergies between an in-country training program and U.S. arms transfers.

In countries facing active insurgent or terrorist threats, U.S. forces in-country can also assist their counterparts in planning and, in some cases, conducting operations. For example, as part of their training syllabus, U.S. forces can show unit commanders how they would go about planning and preparing for a platoon-sized patrol or a company-sized raid in a particular location against an enemy thought to be of a certain strength. As actual operations unfold, U.S. forces can assist in providing the best available information on the location and status of the enemy. They can also offer help in establishing and maintaining tactical communications prior to and during the operation. Secure communication systems that preclude intercept by the

---

[2]The operations of Philippine forces against Abu Sayef Group (ASG) rebels provide a recent example of this. Over the course of several months, U.S. special forces in-country trained with their Philippine counterparts, focusing on individual soldier skills and small-unit tactics. New equipment, including rifles and ammunition, was also provided. U.S. forces also offered assistance in planning patrol operations. The result was more frequent and more effective patrols that led to the freeing of one American hostage and the elimination of several terrorists. Follow-on training missions are planned.

enemy are particularly valuable. In some circumstances, it may be appropriate for U.S. forces to transport host-country units to and from operation areas.[3]

Finally, U.S. forces may be able to provide fire support to friendly units approaching or engaged in combat with terrorist groups. U.S. air forces are especially well suited to this task because of their ability to apply firepower precisely when and where it is needed. The AC-130 gunship is, in many cases, the ideal platform for such missions today, since it combines an array of high-fidelity imaging sensors with weapons that can deliver accurate and sustained firepower of several calibers. In fact, the crew aboard an AC-130 orbiting over a battle may, at times, have a better appreciation of the overall situation than forces engaged on the ground. In addition, airpower in the form of tactical airlift and fire support has proven attractive in these situations because it can bring forces and firepower to bear on the enemy without having to move heavy equipment, such as trucks, armored vehicles, and artillery, over land. Airpower obviates the need to rely upon often primitive ground-transportation infrastructures. It also increases the possibility of gaining tactical surprise by limiting the enemy's ability to observe preparations for an attack.

Of course, political sensitivities may preclude such direct U.S. involvement in counterterrorist operations in other countries. Such sensitivities may operate on both sides. The governments of Pakistan and the Philippines, for example, have asked that U.S. forces not participate in combat operations on their territories, in part because they wish to avoid creating the impression that their sovereignty has been somehow compromised. Likewise, the United States has from time to time refrained from supporting combat operations against terrorist groups in certain countries because Washington wishes to avoid becoming too closely identified with regimes whose human rights records are less than spotless.

Such concerns are unavoidable. As a result, one can envisage a number of situations in which direct U.S. involvement in combined

---

[3]Air Force helicopters used for infiltration and exfiltration of special forces can also provide battlefield medical evacuation capabilities. U.S. capabilities for nighttime medical evacuation by helicopter were said to be particularly valuable to Philippine forces engaged in the hunt for members of the ASG in 2002.

counterterrorist operations would be desirable but one or both sides would like to minimize the profile of U.S. forces. In such circumstances, it would be useful if the Air Force could offer commanders capabilities, such as tactical intelligence and precision fire support, that could be brought to bear without leaving behind "fingerprints" associated with U.S. forces. Certain platforms, such as the Global Hawk unmanned aerial vehicle (UAV), are small enough that they cannot be seen from the ground when at their normal operating altitudes. Likewise, AC-130s or bombers at altitude are difficult for terrorists to detect at night. If well integrated with forces on the ground, such platforms can, in many circumstances, greatly increase the prospects for success in offensive operations against terrorist and insurgent groups while leaving the source of the support ambiguous and unacknowledged.

It must be anticipated that stamping out terrorist activities directed against the United States will require sustained efforts in many countries over a period of years. The U.S. armed forces should thus anticipate a steady demand for long-term training and advisory assistance missions abroad. These missions will call for commissioned and noncommissioned officers (NCOs) who combine high levels of operational expertise with the ability to communicate effectively across cultural and linguistic divides. As U.S. forces develop relationships of professional trust with counterparts abroad, those relationships can be strengthened by increasing foreign attendance at the armed forces' schools for training and education in the United States. The prospect of selection for a year at one of the war colleges, NCO academies, or other schools in the United States can be a strong incentive with which to reward high performers in foreign military organizations.

DISRUPT THE ACTIVITIES OF TERRORISTS

The ultimate objective of military operations against terrorist groups is to eliminate the threat. This will generally require that the most hard-core terrorists be captured or killed—a task that is addressed later in this chapter. Competent foes will make it difficult to locate, identify, and engage them, so successes in this all-important objective will be episodic no matter what the level of resources devoted to the task. But it would be a mistake to think that capturing and killing terrorists is the sole object of counterterrorist military operations.

As noted previously, terrorist groups operating in countries where the government seeks to suppress or destroy them exhibit many of the characteristics of insurgent groups. One of the key lessons of past counterinsurgency efforts is that success depends heavily on the ability of government forces to maintain relentless pressure on the insurgents. If insurgents are permitted to determine the pace of their operations—that is, if they and not the government have the initiative—it is extremely difficult to suppress them because by choosing the time and place to strike, the insurgents can minimize the chances of tactical failure. Conversely, if government forces can keep the insurgents off-balance, many of the insurgents' efforts will be diverted from planning and conducting offensive operations to trying simply to survive and avoid capture. People and groups under pressure for extended periods operate less effectively: they make more mistakes and they may find it more difficult to cooperate and to maintain organizational coherence. Counterinsurgency forces can exploit these openings.

U.S. and host-country forces can do a number of things to advance the objective of subjecting active terrorist groups to constant pressure. Several tasks stand out:

- **Prevent or disrupt recruitment and training.** Prior to September 11, al Qaeda and related groups openly recruited new members not only in Afghanistan but also in Sudan, Pakistan, Somalia, the Philippines, Saudi Arabia, and Yemen. Large training camps were established in several of these countries. Active government efforts to suppress such activities, coupled with plausible threats of U.S. military action, have compelled terrorist groups in some areas to desist from open recruiting and training, reducing the scope of potential future operations.

- **Disrupt communications and databases.** No large organization can operate effectively without reliable communications and record keeping. Aggressive efforts to exploit and interfere with the communication links used by terrorist groups and to corrupt or mine computer files and other records can compel the enemy to adopt less-efficient modes of operation.

- **Interdict the movement of critical materiel and personnel.** Energetic efforts to monitor and interdict the movement of ships, vehicles, aircraft, commercial air passengers, and people on foot through particular areas can be useful in a number of ways. First, such efforts will yield some successes in preventing terrorist groups from acquiring or positioning weapons, explosives, or other materiel needed for their operations. Second, continuous monitoring of traffic on a long-term basis will provide analysts with a picture of what constitutes normal activity, making it easier to detect anomalies. Third, awareness of U.S. and allied interdiction efforts can compel terrorist groups to adopt ways of doing business that are more costly and less efficient than they would like, reducing their overall effectiveness.

- **Protect potential targets.** U.S. military forces, along with advisors from other agencies, can assist foreign governments in identifying and protecting potential targets of terrorist attacks. Although it will never be possible to protect all potential targets, by raising the bar faced by would-be attackers, governments can hope to reduce the number of attacks and their severity, while deflecting terrorists to less-lucrative targets and increasing the odds that would-be perpetrators will be apprehended before they can strike.

ALIENATE TERRORISTS FROM THE POPULACE

Much has been made of the need to "win the hearts and minds" of the populace in the fight against insurgencies and, today, in the global fight against terrorist groups.[4] This emphasis on the perceptions and judgments of the uncommitted is altogether proper. If cut off from the support of the populace by government forces, the terrorists and insurgents find it difficult to move about freely and to gain steady access to such essentials as food, money, housing, and

---

[4]In modern usage, the term (and the strategy) originated with the British campaign against communist insurgents in Malaya after World War II. In the words of Lt. Gen. Sir Gerald Templer, the British High Commissioner to Malaya in the early 1950s, "The shooting side of the business is only 25 percent of the trouble. The other 75 percent is getting the people of this country behind us" (Richard Stubbs, *Hearts and Minds in Guerrilla Warfare: The Malayan Emergency, 1948–1960*, Oxford University Press, Oxford, UK, 1991, p. 259).

information. Conversely, military operations that succeed in destroying today's terrorists would be of little avail if they prompt the emergence of more terrorists to take their places. Indeed, provoking governments into military and police actions that alienate large segments of the population has long been a key objective of terrorist and insurgent violence. If the need to avoid such tactics was important in the 1950s and 1960s, it is even more crucial now that press coverage of U.S. and allied military actions is broadcast globally in near-real time.

In countries faced with active insurgencies or terrorist operations, U.S. and host-country forces can do much to help convince the populace that their interests lie in opposing violent, antigovernment groups. Generally, the most important step is to work vigorously to provide a more secure environment for the civilian population in areas threatened by terrorist or insurgent violence. If a substantial majority believes that the government is capable of protecting them and their families from violence and that the government's forces will treat them fairly, violent opposition groups will find it difficult to secure the support they need. Nothing, in short, succeeds like success. Material incentives, such as job programs, infrastructure development projects, or outright payoffs to local leaders, can be helpful as well. U.S. forces can also make good use of medical and dental professionals to bring benefits to local populations in underserved areas. However, initiatives such as these are generally not effective in and of themselves if the government cannot credibly demonstrate to the people its ability to protect them from insurgent reprisals.

In addition to these positive inducements, U.S. and host-country forces should structure their operations so as to avoid negative consequences. The most obvious of these is collateral damage—unwanted harm to civilians or physical capital from military operations. Moral as well as pragmatic imperatives lie behind the extreme care with which U.S. decisionmakers and military forces plan and conduct military operations. Although absolute perfection in the application of lethal force is unachievable, in recent conflicts in Iraq, the Balkans, and Afghanistan, U.S. air operations have set new standards for both accurate delivery of ordnance and precision in the selection of targets.

Nevertheless, civilian deaths and damage to nonmilitary targets will accompany almost any sizable military operation. Counterinsurgent and counterterrorist operations are particularly prone to creating collateral damage because of the inherent difficulties of locating, identifying, and isolating targets. As horrific as their attacks can be, insurgency and terrorism are ultimately weapons of the weak. And being weak, the perpetrators of these attacks must shield themselves from the power of states by blending into the physical landscape or civilian society. Thus, restraint in the application of force in counterterrorist operations is essential. One U.S. Air Force officer who was a member of the planning staff at the Combined Air Operations Center during Operation Enduring Freedom put it succinctly, stating, "Bad bombs make more terrorists." Avoiding harm to civilians is partly a matter of exercising care in the conduct of operations. It is also a matter of accumulating accurate intelligence and equipping forces with weapons appropriate to the counterterrorist/counterinsurgency environment—two topics addressed later.

U.S. forces must also be wary of the possibility of "cultural" collateral damage associated with their deployment and operations abroad. That is, their activities should be managed so as to minimize antagonizing people in the host country. This includes operational activities, such as conducting search operations and manning checkpoints, as well as unofficial activities, including off-duty contacts with the local population. In a similar vein, U.S. policy generally should be that the role of U.S. forces in fighting terrorist groups abroad is to support host-government operations. If the U.S. contribution to combined operations becomes so substantial as to dwarf the government's own efforts, Washington will be seen as bearing responsibility for the overall campaign, including the actions of host-country forces over which it actually might exercise little or no control. In most circumstances, it is far better if the host-country government takes and keeps "ownership" of the problem.

Finally, U.S. and allied information and psychological operations can be helpful by discrediting the terrorists. Such operations have two primary audiences. The most important audience is civilian populations that might otherwise be sympathetic to the terrorists. The other is the terrorists themselves or their supporters who might not be as fully committed to the cause as their leaders. With respect to the broader audience, the objective is to convince people that the terrorists do not have their best interests at heart, that what they are doing is morally unjustified, that they are pursuing a selfish set of objectives, and, in so doing, they are worsening the lot of Muslims (or other target audiences) everywhere. With respect to the less-committed terrorist, the object is to encourage defection, both by driving a psychological wedge between the rank and file and the leadership and by offering promise of fair treatment to those who surrender. In all cases, information campaigns will be most effective when the messages they convey are consistent with the conduct of other military operations.[5]

GATHER INTELLIGENCE ABOUT TERRORIST NETWORKS AND ACTIVITIES

A worldwide effort to collect, evaluate, and integrate intelligence about terrorist networks will be the centerpiece of U.S. and allied efforts to defeat terrorist groups with global reach. Any single operation undertaken by U.S. forces, whether on a large scale, such as in Operation Enduring Freedom in Afghanistan, or a small scale, such as in the training mission in Yemen, will have as a core purpose not only the achievement of objectives specific to that country but also the development of a clearer picture of anti-Western terrorist groups and operations worldwide. For this reason, and because accurate and timely information about the enemy is so crucial to successful counterterrorist operations in any setting, the Department of Defense and the Air Force in particular should expect high levels of demand for surveillance platforms and for analysis of the "take" of these platforms for the indefinite future.

As with any operation against covert organizations, "human intelligence" (HUMINT)—information provided by human informants—will be critical. Much of this information will be gathered by operatives outside of the U.S. armed forces, often working closely with the intelligence services of the host country. However, U.S. special operations forces (SOF) and regular forces will also develop sources of information about the local situation in the course of their operations.

---

[5]For more on the integration of psychological operations and air operations, see Stephen T. Hosmer, *Psychological Effects of U.S. Air Operations in Four Wars, 1941–1991*, RAND, MR-576-AF, 1996, especially pp. 199–202.

Integrating the information developed from HUMINT with other forms of intelligence will be essential to success. HUMINT can provide vital contextual information about terrorist groups and can be used to cue technical collection means to focus on particular targets to develop a fuller picture of the situation. Likewise, information from technical sensors can be used to focus HUMINT collection efforts on potentially lucrative areas or topics.

New generations of sensors will improve the ability of U.S. forces to detect and monitor the activities of small groups of enemy combatants. For example, the Air Force is developing a new synthetic aperture radar (SAR) that operates simultaneously in the ultra high frequency (UHF) and very high frequency (VHF) bands and can detect stationary targets under foliage or camouflage. These sensors will not provide the resolution required for identifying (or perhaps even detecting) individuals, but they can be used to detect facilities and equipment (including weapons) that might be associated with terrorist groups and activities.

Improving assessment capabilities is also important. Most of the images and other data collected by U.S. intelligence sensors are never looked at or are given only a cursory examination. To better exploit the burgeoning "take" of these sensors, efforts are under way to develop new automated assessment tools that will include computer algorithms designed to detect specific activities by, say, people or vehicles and to detect anomalous events or activities against an established baseline.

PROTECT FRIENDLY FORCES AND BASES

Protecting U.S. forces and assets worldwide from terrorist attacks is always a high priority, but concern for the safety of U.S. forces increases when those forces are deployed in a region close to the home base of one or more terrorist groups. Deploying forces abroad for extended periods is essential to providing effective training and advisory assistance to friendly forces and for supporting other components of a comprehensive counterterrorism strategy. Commanders must take steps to ensure that such deployments do not provide greater opportunities for terrorists to attack Americans.

This imperative has a number of implications for the conduct of military operations abroad. First, of course, bases of operations must be chosen with care and with an eye toward defensibility. The ability to control access onto the base is a vital prerequisite of security. Another is the ability to monitor and patrol areas outside of the base's perimeter so as to enforce restrictions on activities within these areas. Terrorist and insurgent groups typically have access to sniper rifles, rocket-propelled grenades, and mortars, which can allow them to attack personnel at ranges of up to several kilometers. Likewise, large truck bombs can kill people in buildings hundreds of feet away, as the terrorists who attacked U.S. forces residing in Khobar Towers in Saudi Arabia demonstrated.

Threats such as these underscore the importance of gathering intelligence about the activities and capabilities of terrorist groups. HUMINT assets and liaison activities with local security organizations must assess potential threats to U.S. forces as well as the broader challenges posed by terrorist groups in the area of operations. Technical surveillance systems, such as electro-optical sensors on UAVs, may be useful for this purpose as well.

The problem of emphasizing force-protection measures is that such concerns can begin to compete with the overall mission of neutralizing terrorist groups. To reduce the severity of this competition, the Department of Defense will need to develop and field affordable systems appropriate for monitoring activities around friendly bases. Fairly simple, low-cost systems could be adequate to this task. For example, small, low-speed UAVs with a time-on-station of a few hours have proven to be quite suitable for base-protection missions and are much less expensive than a Predator UAV. Unattended ground sensors (UGSs) may be useful for these tasks as well. They tend to have a smaller field of regard than sensors on airborne platforms, but they are relatively inexpensive and are on station 24 hours a day. Scanning lasers can be used to detect rifle scopes and other optics pointed at a base, and infrared backtracking systems can identify the source of sniper fire. Both systems can be useful in protecting forces and bases.[6]

---

[6]For more on concepts for countering snipers, see Alan Vick et al., *Aerospace Operations in Urban Environments: Exploring New Concepts*, RAND, MR-1187-AF, 2000, pp. 131–138.

FIND AND CAPTURE OR KILL TERRORISTS

As was noted above, the ultimate aim of operations against terrorist groups is to eliminate the threat. Operation Enduring Freedom, which rid Afghanistan of the Taliban regime and prompted many Taliban and al Qaeda members to flee the country, suggests that the more successful U.S. and allied efforts against terrorist groups are, the more difficult it could be to find, identify, and root out remaining elements of the network. Terrorists who survive efforts to destroy them will adapt by presenting ever smaller "signatures" that might be used to locate and identify them. Accordingly, U.S. forces and their counterparts abroad will continue to be engaged in hunting for very small groups of people and, ultimately, individuals.

This situation presents a somewhat novel set of challenges for airmen, although the trend toward ever more discrete target sets has been discernable for some time. As Table 1 shows, the focus or "level

Table 1

Targets of U.S. Combat Air Operations

Era	Targets
Pre-WWII	Cities
WWII	Installations
Vietnam	Installations Bridges Fielded forces
Gulf War	Buildings and bridges Armored vehicles
Serbia/Kosovo	Portions of buildings Vehicles within convoys Troop concentrations
Afghanistan	Individual vehicles Houses within villages Individuals

of resolution" of U.S. air operations has become steadily finer since airpower's inception as an instrument of war. Prior to World War II, aerial bombardment was regarded primarily as an instrument of mass terror; its targets were cities and the people and infrastructure within them. At the same time, theorists and practitioners in the United States Army Air Corps were developing the doctrine of day-light precision bombardment. The objective here was to destroy key elements of an enemy's war-supporting industrial base so as to render continued military operations impossible. Although enemy air defenses and shortcomings in bombing accuracy made it difficult to implement this theory, the aspiration for conducting more-focused attacks remained and some success was achieved, particularly against Nazi Germany.

The dominant role of nuclear weapons in U.S. defense strategy in the 1950s retarded the development of more-accurate conventional delivery capabilities, but the Vietnam War reminded defense planners of the need to be able to destroy an enemy's war-making potential by means of air attacks using conventional weapons. As the first "televised war," Vietnam also pointed to the growing importance of being able to limit collateral damage. Not coincidentally, laser-guided bombs were developed and first used during the Vietnam conflict. The Gulf War, however, was the first time that precision-guided munitions (PGMs) were used on a large scale. The availability of large numbers of PGM-capable fighter-bombers,[7] combined with the fact that coalition air forces were able to achieve air supremacy over Iraq within the first few days of the war, meant that far more precision was possible and expected from U.S. and allied air operations. Now individual buildings or, in many cases, specific portions of buildings were chosen for attack.

This trend accelerated in Operations Deliberate Force and Allied Force—the efforts to bring an end to Serbian aggression in Bosnia and Kosovo, respectively. Particularly in Operation Allied Force, where no organized friendly ground force was engaged, airpower was

---

[7]U.S. air forces deployed to Operation Desert Storm included more than 250 fixed-wing aircraft that were capable of delivering laser-guided bombs. They were supplemented by several squadrons of British Tornadoes and a handful of other PGM-capable allied aircraft.

called upon to suppress atrocities being committed against civilians and to put coercive pressure on the Serbian leadership. Targets included buildings in urban areas, small groups of soldiers within villages, and individual vehicles within convoys. The same sorts of targets have been prominent in Operation Enduring Freedom in Afghanistan. There, U.S. air forces have had some success in locating and attacking small groups of terrorists, particularly when trained tactical air controllers have been available to assist in identifying targets and providing attack platforms with target coordinates.

Perhaps the most intriguing new capability to be demonstrated in Afghanistan is the armed Predator UAV. The small size and quiet engine of the Predator make it difficult for people on the ground to detect even when it is directly overhead. These features, coupled with an endurance on station approaching 24 hours, have allowed operators to track potential targets for extended periods. The Hellfire missile carried by the Predator permits accurate attacks on individual vehicles or small groups of people in clear weather, using laser-homing guidance.

Nevertheless, ferreting out individuals or small groups of terrorists, positively identifying them, and engaging them without harming nearby civilians is an extremely demanding task. Substantial improvements will be needed in several areas before the Air Force can be confident of being able to provide this capability to combatant commanders.

PREVENT TERRORISTS FROM ACQUIRING, RETAINING, OR USING CBRN WEAPONS

Chemical, biological, radiological, and nuclear weapons in the hands of rogue governments or terrorist groups present a special challenge that transcends individual operations in particular countries. Because CBRN weapons have the potential to allow small groups of determined individuals to kill hundreds or thousands of people in a single attack, U.S. leaders will place a high priority on developing capabilities for defeating such threats. U.S. strategy recognizes that not all adversaries will be deterred by traditional means—by the threat to inflict unacceptable damage in retaliation for enemy attacks. This is particularly true of terrorist groups such as al Qaeda, whose raison d'etre is essentially to harm Americans and which present little in the way of infrastructure that could be targeted by a retaliatory strike. Deterrent threats can be used to help dissuade governments from providing CBRN weapons to terrorist groups. But ultimately, our primary defense against such weapons in the hands of terrorists is to try to prevent such groups from obtaining, retaining, or using them. Accordingly, U.S. forces may be called upon at any time to counter the threat of such weapons.

A wide range of complementary approaches is called for to address this threat. Many of these, such as programs to secure fissile material and chemical weapons, provide secure employment for nuclear scientists and engineers, and monitor cargo coming into the United States, draw primarily on resources outside of the Department of Defense. Military forces and assets are chiefly responsible for striving to determine which groups are seeking to acquire CBRN weapons, denying them access to those weapons, and foiling attempts to retain, position, or release them. The small size of the weapons in relation to their destructive power makes these tasks extremely demanding. Like many other aspects of the effort to defeat terrorist threats, this one places a premium on accurate and timely intelligence: locating and correctly identifying the weapons constitutes the most challenging aspect of the problem.

Chapter Three

TOWARD NEW CONCEPTS FOR LOCATING AND ATTACKING TERRORISTS AND RELATED TARGETS

Notwithstanding the successes that U.S. and allied forces have had in disrupting terrorist operations in and around Afghanistan, serious shortfalls remain. Specifically, improvements are called for in the capabilities of U.S. air forces to locate, identify, and attack very small groups of people with appropriate levels of confidence that the right target is being attacked and that innocent civilians will not be placed at undue risk. What opportunities might exist to define new and more effective concepts of execution (CONEXs) for engaging such targets?

We must first recognize that terrorists will try to operate in areas and ways that make them difficult to find, identify, and isolate. Depending on the country in which they are operating, they may be in wilderness areas that feature mountains, caves, forest, or jungle canopy. They may be living in rural areas, using anonymous-looking dwellings or small encampments. They may choose urban environments, again occupying unexceptional buildings. Within these environments, terrorists may be either stationary or moving, with movement being by vehicle or on foot. In all cases, the terrorists may be in the company of noncombatants—either family members or unrelated strangers. Any new concept for engaging such a demanding target set should seek to incorporate innovations among "finders, controllers, and shooters."

WIDE-AREA SURVEILLANCE

"Finders"—intelligence, reconnaissance, and surveillance assets—will be of two broad types: those that provide wide-area coverage and those with a narrow field of view but higher resolution. The role of wide-area assets will be to provide information about the overall operations of targeted groups and to identify those areas that might merit more intensive investigation. Assets available today include networks of human informants (HUMINT), signals intelligence collectors (SIGINT), and imaging sensors that provide pictures of potential targets. Each of these types of assets has its strengths and limitations. A severe limitation of most imagery sensors is their inability to see through heavy foliage—a major problem in countries such as the Philippines that are heavily forested. Foliage penetration SAR and moving-target indication (MTI) radars, which have been under development for several years, could significantly enhance U.S. wide-area surveillance capabilities in such regions, helping to find objects that merit reexamination using a higher-resolution sensor.

Emerging technologies for multispectral and hyperspectral sensors will make it possible to remotely examine phenomena across the electromagnetic spectrum. Because every material has a unique signature, data from such sensors can be processed and used to classify objects automatically and with greater fidelity than is possible with sensors that operate in only a single waveband. By comparing this information against a database of objects of interest, analysts using appropriate algorithms can sort through masses of data quickly to locate objects and activities that merit closer examination.[1]

Other promising technologies with the potential to enhance wide-area search capabilities are chemical "sniffers." Essentially miniature, mobile chemical-analysis laboratories, sniffers are able to detect traces of certain chemicals in the atmosphere. If it were possible to develop sniffers to detect particular types of explosives, then low-flying aircraft or ground vehicles could patrol large areas and

---

[1]For an overview of emerging sensor technologies and their potential to support operations against dispersed groups of enemy personnel, see Alan Vick et al., *Enhancing Airpower's Contribution Against Light Infantry Targets*, RAND, MR-697-AF, 1996, pp. 13–30.

highlight places where bomb factories, arms caches, or potential suicide bombers might be operating. Stocks of chemical weapons or precursor materials might also be detectable. In addition, certain types of illegal drugs or the chemicals used in their processing might be useful targets for sniffers, given the nexus between drug traffickers and terrorists in some areas (e.g., Colombia). Miniature UAVs could carry spectrometers and sample-collection/analysis devices, transmitting data or returning physical samples back to a "mother ship" or a ground station.

HIGH-RESOLUTION SENSORS

Sensors employed for wide-area searches help analysts to gain a clearer picture of the nature of the enemy's organization and operations and to identify places where other human and technical assets can be concentrated in hopes of gaining confirmation of the presence or absence of the enemy and, perhaps, the identity of individual terrorists. Such sensors, be they human sources or technical means, ideally should provide continuous monitoring of suspect areas and persons. They should also be covert; that is, able to function without tipping off targets that they are under surveillance.

These requirements—high resolution, continuous and long-term coverage, and secrecy—suggest that sensors to support targeting should, in general, be small so that they can be easily concealed. Small imaging sensors, in turn, must be placed close to their targets, given the need for high resolution and restrictions on focal length.[2] And sensors that need to "stare" at their targets for prolonged periods should generally not be on airborne platforms but rather placed on buildings or other fixed structures, or in trees.[3]

---

[2]For a review of the current state of the art in imaging sensor technologies and their potential for miniaturization, see Alan Vick et al., 2000, pp. 83–107.

[3]In some situations, such sensors can be emplaced by agents on the ground. In others, delivery by air might be preferred. The Internetted Unattended Ground Sensor (IUGS) program, initiated by the Defense Advanced Research Projects Agency, is developing an air-delivered body with magnetic, seismic, acoustic, chemical, and environmental sensors that can detect human and vehicular movements. See Alan Vick et al., 1996, pp. 26–27.

As noted previously, automated processing tools are being developed to help analysts more efficiently screen the masses of data being gathered by new generations of sensors. Such tools are especially important in counterterrorist operations because the signatures associated with most terrorist groups are generally very small and the "noise" surrounding them is often considerable. For example, U.S. and Pakistani officials today are attempting to apprehend perhaps several hundred individuals in the city of Karachi, which has a population in excess of five million. Under such circumstances, a surveillance and identification system that boasted an error rate of only 1:1000 could still give off many false alarms for each correct identification.

Conventional cameras cannot see inside buildings if the occupants are cautious and if it is not possible to plant devices inside. One means of gaining information about activities inside a building is to listen to what is being said there. Occasionally, it may be possible to plant listening devices ("bugs") in buildings or vehicles being used by terrorists. More often, antiterrorist forces will have to rely on remote means of monitoring. It has been demonstrated that one can sometimes listen in on conversations inside a building by using lasers to detect the propagation of sound waves off the building's windows.

Experiments are also under way with radars that have the potential to "see" through walls. The resolution of such radars is, of course, modest, but it is possible to determine whether particular rooms in a structure are occupied or not—information that can be valuable when planning an attack. Another emerging technology that can be useful in identifying terrorists is facial-recognition software. If cameras can be placed in areas where terrorists might pass by, the images they collect could be rapidly screened against a database of facial images and perhaps other physical characteristics of known terrorists. Computer algorithms capable of comparing collected images against a large database and discriminating among key features of those images will be essential if this approach is to be effective. Even with these systems, additional efforts would be required to verify the identity of potential targets, given the large number of samples collected and likely false-alarm rates.

Tagging suspected vehicles could help in developing information about patterns of activity and assisting shooters in engaging elusive targets. For example, an operative on the ground in a city could covertly place a transmitter on a car that is being used by a group suspected of conducting terrorist activities. Once attached, the transmitter could permit authorities to monitor that vehicle's movements, perhaps pointing them to other groups of terrorists. Signals from the transmitter could also make it easier to keep the suspect vehicle "in the crosshairs" should a decision be taken to detain its occupants or destroy it.

DYNAMIC ENGAGEMENT CONTROL

Mediating between the finders and the shooters is a critical function that could be termed dynamic engagement control. These days, aircrews in shooter platforms may not have as clear or comprehensive a picture of the battlefield situation as those in control centers where information from multiple sensors is being gathered and evaluated. People in these centers—operational controllers—must manage the sensors and shooters to best use their capabilities in response to a dynamic situation. Others, called tactical controllers, direct shooters to engage particular targets and provide them with the information they need to conduct the engagement effectively.   Tactical controllers generally are not located in the operations center with operational controllers but rather are closer to the action. For example, the tactical control teams on the ground with Northern Alliance units in Afghanistan gave target coordinates to aircraft attacking Taliban forces and thus performed this function. Tactical controllers can also reside on Airborne Warning and Control System (AWACS) and Joint Surveillance and Target Attack Radar System (JSTARS) aircraft. If air forces are to be successful in hunting down small groups of terrorists, a tactical controller generally will be needed to direct and assist shooters in engaging these elusive targets.

The work of tactical air controllers can be greatly facilitated by the availability of (1) accurate data on the location of targets, (2) secure data links to shooters, and (3) avionics in the cockpits of attack aircraft to permit aircrews to best use the data and direction provided. Generations of forward air controllers have had to rely on the art of "talking the pilot's eyes onto the target" to prosecute effective attacks. In many circumstances, this demanding and time-consuming process is prone to error. The advent of the Global Positioning

System (GPS) allows controllers to locate targets quickly and with great precision. Equally important, GPS allows aircrews to know their own locations precisely, to slew on-board sensors onto the designated target, and to direct guided weapons to their aimpoints. Data link communications between controllers and shooters facilitate efficient attack operations by eliminating several potential sources of delay and error in passing target coordinates by voice to aircrews and then translating these coordinates into digital commands within the aircraft's avionics. In some circumstances, data links can also allow digitized images of targets and the surrounding environment to be sent to shooter aircraft.

THE WEAPON

The final piece of the CONEX is the weapon or munition. U.S. air forces have made great strides over the past two decades or so in the precise delivery of firepower. Laser-guided bombs (LGBs) can be delivered within a few feet of their intended targets with great reliability. And the Joint Direct Attack Munition (JDAM), by exploiting GPS, provides accuracy close to that of an LGB in all weather conditions, without requiring the aircrew delivering the weapon to acquire the target visually. What is lacking in the Air Force's inventory of air-to-ground weapons are weapons at the low end of the lethality spectrum and weapons that can be effective in densely built-up and populated areas.

The general-purpose bombs that make up the bulk of the Air Force's inventory of air-to-ground weapons weigh between 500 and 2000 pounds. Dropped from altitude, weapons of this size release tremendous kinetic energy on impact. When even the smallest of them detonates, it can be lethal to unprotected humans over an area of tens of thousands of square feet. The weapons are thus ideal for destroying buildings or attacking troops in the open but poorly suited to attacks on terrorists hiding or moving among civilians. For these cases, much smaller warheads are called for. The Hellfire missile, which has a warhead weighing about 20 pounds, is more appropriate for such applications. In good weather, when an aircraft at medium altitude can see the target on the ground, Hellfire may be the weapon of choice for attacking individuals in a vehicle or in a large room within a particular building. However, its laser homing guidance system would be ineffective in overcast conditions or fog, and even its 20-pound warhead would be too large for attacking people in the open who might be surrounded by innocent civilians. Even the 2.75-inch rocket, which has a warhead about half the size of the Hellfire's, would place people at risk over an area of several thousand square feet.[4]

The ideal weapon for hunting down individual terrorists or small groups in cities, towns, or villages would have a warhead weighing only one to two pounds. A warhead of this size, accurately delivered, would provide a high probability of kill against individuals or small groups in the open, but it would pose little threat to people 30 to 40 feet away. The weapon should be command guided via an electro-optical sensor and a data link to the delivering aircraft. The aircrew could place the crosshairs on the desired aimpoint and view the target through the weapon's sensor, confirming the location and general appearance of the target, if not its identity. The data link between the weapon and the aircrew employing it would also permit the warhead to be designed with a "fail-safe" mechanism, allowing the aircrew to disable the explosive charge if there were last-minute uncertainties about the engagement.

The delivery vehicle for this warhead could be a small glide vehicle with wings that deploy after release from the aircraft. If delivered from medium altitude, such a vehicle could glide 20 nautical miles or more. A small rocket motor could be used in the final phase of the engagement to ensure that the weapon had sufficient energy to make any necessary terminal maneuvers or to reattack if required. The vehicle should fly at a fairly low speed (approximately 100 kn) and have control surfaces that allow it to be maneuvered through urban terrain. Such a weapon would give commanders capabilities to attack terrorists in a variety of situations when ground forces might not be readily available or when employing them would entail unacceptable risks.

An alternative concept would place the sensor and warhead on a small, expendable hovering vehicle delivered by air. Such a vehicle would provide a better platform for observing the target, with im-

---

[4]The 2.75-inch rocket is an unguided weapon and is therefore not appropriate for precision attacks in any case. It could, however, be fitted with a laser guidance kit.

agery again being sent by data link to the controlling aircrew. Its kill mechanism could be an explosively forged slug or fragmentation warhead that is aimed at the target when detonated.

DESTROYING STOCKS OF CBRN WEAPONS

Many of the concepts for wide-area surveillance mentioned earlier in this chapter would be relevant as well in the search for CBRN weapons that may be in the hands of terrorists or rogue governments. As with every aspect of counterterrorist operations, HUMINT—including efforts to infiltrate enemy organizations—will be particularly relevant. Sniffers capable of detecting certain chemical or biological agents have also been mentioned in this regard. Nuclear weapons and radiological material, of course, emit a variety of radioactive signatures associated with nuclear decay. The trick is to detect these from extended ranges—a serious technical challenge given the enemy's likely efforts to conceal such signatures and the background radiation present in the environment. It might also prove difficult to distinguish between signatures associated with weapons and those from legitimate sources, such as nuclear materials associated with medical treatments. To reduce the probability of detection and to make attacking their weapons more difficult, a number of regimes have resorted to building facilities deep underground. The proliferation of such facilities greatly complicates U.S. efforts to locate and destroy CBRN weapons. Earth-penetrating radars, which could be mounted on airborne platforms, have some potential for revealing the outlines of underground structures, but it is unlikely that the radars can be made to penetrate very far or to image the contents of underground structures.

Where it is suspected that CBRN weapons are being stored underground, military planners will have two broad options for trying to eliminate the threat posed by these weapons—strike and seizure. The strike option calls for weapons delivered by aircraft or missiles that can (1) penetrate many feet of earth and reinforced concrete and detonate reliably or (2) seal off access to the facility for a sustained period. Work is proceeding to design improved conventional weapons and specialized, low-yield nuclear warheads for these purposes. For attacks on chemical and biological weapons, it will be important not only to destroy the facility housing the weapons but also to neutralize the lethal agents themselves so they are not vented into the surrounding environment. High-temperature fuel-air explosives might be one means of accomplishing both goals. A low-yield nuclear explosion might have similar effects, although it would present contamination risks of its own. There has also been speculation about the existence of high-powered microwave warheads that use an explosive charge to generate a short, intense burst of electromagnetic energy sufficient to destroy electrical circuitry within a circumscribed range. If practical, such weapons might be used to disable the fuzing mechanisms of CBRN warheads, rendering them unusable for a period of time.

Terrorist groups seeking to develop, hide, or move CBRN weapons might well lack sophisticated facilities such as underground bunkers, relying instead on innocuous-looking warehouses or private dwellings in built-up areas or caves in sparsely populated regions to mask their activities and weapons. Sensors that operate at fairly short ranges might be useful against targets such as these.

Seizing CBRN weapons or gaining control of the area around a weapon-storage facility can present challenges as well. If a nation possessed such weapons and threatened to use them, a large-scale military operation might be warranted. Such an operation would aim to defeat the enemy nation's military forces, take down the regime, and occupy the country, gaining control of the CBRN weapons in the process. The difficulty with this approach, aside from the costs and risks attendant to any large-scale conflict, is that the enemy would presumably have time to disperse stocks of CBRN weapons, deploy some or all of them with forces in the field, and use them against U.S. forces in the theater and against neighboring countries. For these reasons, decisionmakers will be interested in capabilities that enable the destruction or seizure of CBRN weapons before they can be dispersed, either in the opening stage of a much larger military campaign or in a separate commando-style operation.

One serious shortfall in U.S. special operations capabilities today is the lack of a means for inserting and extracting SOF teams stealthily. SOF helicopters and C-130 cargo planes are equipped for low-level operations, but if they fly within line of sight of radars they can be readily detected and tracked. Because surprise and survivability are such important elements of successful SOF operations, the Air Force should explore concepts for a stealthy medium transport aircraft. To be of use to SOF in a wide range of scenarios, such an aircraft could be somewhat smaller than the C-130, which has a payload of around 40,000 pounds. But it would need to have a mission radius of 1000 miles or so to permit operations deep within the territory of hostile countries. Equally important, this SOF transport should be capable of landing at and taking off from short, unimproved airstrips or highway segments.[5]

A transport aircraft with these features might also prove to be well suited to serving as a successor to the AC-130 gunship. Developing a more-survivable gunship should be a priority because surface-to-air missiles capable of downing the AC-130 are proliferating and SOF and other light forces often require the type of sustained, precise fire support that the AC-130 provides.

_____

[5]The Air Force Special Operations Command (AFSOC) is committed to procuring some 50 V-22 Osprey tilt-rotor aircraft. These vertical takeoff and landing machines will replace some of AFSOC's helicopter fleet, offering greater speed and range, but they are not stealthy and cannot substitute for the C-130 in delivering large payloads over ranges greater than a few hundred miles.

Chapter Four

THE NEW "STEADY STATE": IMPLICATIONS FOR FORCE PLANNING

THE DEMANDS OF A WAR ON TERRORISM

The imperative to monitor, suppress, attack, and ultimately eradicate international terrorist groups seeking to strike the United States, its citizens, its interests, and its allies is prompting significant changes in the demands placed on the armed forces of the United States, including the Air Force. Many of these changes will remain prominent features of the security environment for years to come.

As of this writing in early 2003, U.S. and allied forces operating in and around Afghanistan have not succeeded in capturing or killing a number of al Qaeda's leaders, many of its fighters, and any number of virulently anti-Western radicals willing and able to use violence to advance their cause. Nevertheless, Operation Enduring Freedom has succeeded in eliminating what had been al Qaeda's primary sanctuary prior to September 11. This fact, combined with an assessment of other potential venues for counterterrorist military operations, suggests that the "war" on terrorism in the future is likely to look much less like a war than Operation Enduring Freedom did in the fall and winter of 2001–2002.

Figure 2 depicts a continuum along which is plotted a range of types of military operations that could be undertaken against terrorist groups in a particular country. The left side of the continuum, "Over the horizon," includes operations in which U.S. military involvement is minimal. Here, U.S. forces are collecting information on the

31

activities or terrorists using sensors and platforms based outside the target country, passing relevant information to appropriate authorities in that country's government, and incorporating the information into a database of terrorist networks and activities worldwide. The far right-hand side of the figure, by contrast, includes operations in which U.S. forces, some of which may be based inside the target country, are engaged in fairly large-scale combat operations against terrorists based there. Between these two extremes are operations in which small numbers of U.S. forces are in the target country, are providing training to host-country forces ("Train and equip"), and may be participating to some degree in antiterrorist operations conducted by host-country forces ("Support during operations").

Arrayed along this continuum are the names of selected countries where U.S. forces have been operating since September 11 or where U.S. counterterrorist operations could be undertaken in the future. As the figure shows, we judge that Operation Enduring Freedom represents an example of U.S. forces undertaking large-scale military operations against terrorist groups in another country. Only Somalia, because of the weak nature of its transitional government and the possibility that elements of its population might play willing hosts to al Qaeda and similar groups, looks like a potential venue for similar operations in the near future. In other plausible cases that we have identified, the roles played by U.S. military forces will most often be indirect and supportive, for a variety of reasons.

RAND*MR1738-2*

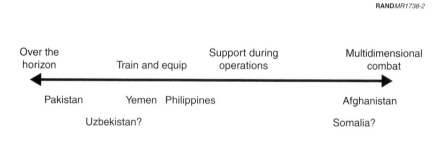

Figure 2—A Spectrum of Counterterrorist Operations

Table 2 highlights this finding. The columns encompass the major types of roles that U.S. military forces might play in countering terrorist groups and activities abroad. Each row shows the author's judgments regarding roles that are likely to be called for in specific cases—some actual and some potential. The table suggests that large-scale operations (such as Enduring Freedom), which involve U.S. forces in the full range of counterterrorist activities, including combat, are likely to be few and far between. On the other hand, the Air Force and the other services can expect widespread and sustained demand for forces and assets capable of gathering information about terrorist operations, assisting friendly forces (at least indirectly) in the conduct of counterterrorist operations, training and advising those forces, and protecting U.S. forces and bases abroad from attack.

The fight against terrorist groups with global reach, in short, looks more like a long "twilight conflict," as the Cold War was once described, than a series of operations involving U.S. forces in sustained or large-scale combat operations. This is not to say that the fight will be easy or risk-free; far from it. But it will call for capabilities that have not, by and large, been at the forefront of U.S. planning and resource allocation for large-scale combat operations.

U.S. forces should expect to be involved in planning and conducting a series of long-term operations by small, tailored packages of forces in areas generally devoid of permanent U.S. military bases. The immediate purpose of these efforts will be to improve the effectiveness of host-country military forces in suppressing and eliminating terrorist activities on their own soil. Accordingly, U.S. forces engaged in these operations will experience extensive interactions with host-country forces, government personnel (including law enforcement and intelligence agencies), and the populace.

The Air Force, then, should expect sustained heavy demands for the following sorts of capabilities:

- Surveillance platforms, operators, and analysts

- Language-qualified personnel—commissioned as well as enlisted—to help train and advise host-country forces, interact with others in-country, and analyze the intelligence "take" from HUMINT and communications intelligence (COMINT) sources

Table 2

Dimensions of U.S. Involvement in Selected Counterrerrorist Operations

					Roles of USAF Forces					
Country	Target Group	Probable Numbers of Terrorists	Collect Intelligence	Train, Advise	Assist During Operations[a]	Strike	Civil Affairs	Combat Search and Rescue	Psyops	Force Protection
Afghanistan (post-Taliban)	al Qaeda, Taliban	1000+	√	√	√	√	√	√	√	√
Pakistan	al Qaeda, Taliban	Hundreds	√		?					√
Philippines	Abu Sayyaf	100–200	√	√	√		√	√		√
Yemen	IAA, YIJ	Several hundred	√	√	?	?	?	?	?	√
Uzbekistan/ Fergana Valley	IMU	Hundreds	√	?	√					√
Somalia	AIAI	~1000	√	?	?	√	√	√	?	√

NOTES: IAA = Islamic Army of Aden
YIJ = Yemen Islamic Jihad
IMU = Islamic Movement of Uzbekistan
AIAI = Al Ittibad Al Islamiya.

[a]Includes intelligence, planning, communications, tactical mobility, and/or airborne fire support.

- Security police and other force-protection assets

- Base operating support personnel and equipment to provide vital functions, such as communications, housing, and transportation at a wide range of locations

- Heliborne insertion and extraction capabilities

- Humanitarian relief assets, including engineers, doctors and dentists, public health specialists, tactical airlift aircraft, and crews.

From time to time, USAF units will be called upon to attack terrorist targets (to include stocks of CBRN weapons) directly. Such attacks could take place in conjunction with host-country or U.S. ground forces, or against targets where no friendly ground forces are engaged. The former types of attacks will require close coordination with engaged ground forces to minimize the possibility of fratricide. In both cases, great care will be required to avoid inflicting harm on innocent civilians.

CONCLUDING OBSERVATIONS

Notwithstanding the horror that terrorist attacks can create, terrorism remains a tactic of the weak. Given the prominent role played by the United States globally and the dominant military capabilities U.S. forces have demonstrated, it is not surprising that terrorist threats have become an increasing concern of U.S. defense planners. Very few states have the military and economic wherewithal to confront the United States and its allies directly in a conventional military contest. Still less can subnational or transnational entities, such as al Qaeda, hope to achieve their objectives by challenging U.S. or allied military power head-on. In addition, the worldwide diffusion of technology is placing ever-greater levels of destructive power within reach of individuals and small groups. For these reasons, we must expect that the nation will continue to confront challenges of an unconventional nature, as adversaries seek to advance their agendas by threatening or employing violence against U.S. and allied interests in ways that are difficult to anticipate, to defeat, or to retaliate against. We must, in short, assume that terror attacks on "soft" civilian targets as well as military forces and installations in the

United States and abroad will remain a prominent feature of the international landscape unless vigorous actions are taken to combat the threat.

The governments of the civilized world will succeed against the threat posed by terrorists only when it becomes abundantly clear to all but the most deranged individuals that terrorism does not pay. This resolution will entail two distinct but related dimensions: First, of course, terrorists themselves must be hunted down and captured or killed. Success in this dimension will have the dual benefit of reducing the number of people striving to attack us and of dissuading others from following in the footsteps of those who have failed in their efforts to attack Americans and their allies.

Second, governments committed to defeating terrorists must demonstrate that continued attacks will only strengthen their determination to press the fight against terrorism. Part of the logic that seems to motivate members of al Qaeda and related groups is the perception that terrorist attacks can compel a government to change its policies if those attacks can inflict sufficiently high levels of casualties. The war on terrorists must have as an objective to convince terrorists and their sympathizers that, when Americans are confronted with a threat to their core values and their way of life, the relationship between casualties and the nation's determination is, in fact, the opposite of that perception.

Complicating efforts to achieve such objectives is the ever-present imperative to avoid actions, such as heavy-handed or indiscriminate military operations, that would exacerbate the threat. The audience for the struggle between terrorists and the civilized world is global. Hence, every aspect of the fight against terrorism must be conducted so as to strengthen the moral standing of the United States and its partners vis-à-vis their terrorist foes.

As this study has stated, military power is only one component of the portfolio of instruments that the nation must bring to bear in the fight against terrorist groups. However, military capabilities play unique and crucial roles in the overall strategy, chiefly in seeking to deny terrorist groups safe haven in countries that might be unwilling or unable to act effectively against those groups. Counterterrorist operations, if conducted over an extended period and on a scale commensurate with the threats we envisage, will call for capabilities that differ, both qualitatively and quantitatively, from the mix of capabilities that the U.S. armed forces has fielded today. The tasks of finding, identifying, and apprehending or killing terrorists, and of destroying stocks of chemical, biological, radiological, and nuclear weapons will call for the development of new concepts incorporating new technologies and systems. Perhaps equally challenging, the tasks of training and advising the forces of friendly governments, of winning hearts and minds, and of protecting U.S. forces and interests around the world will call for investments in people, systems, and operations that, in many cases, lie outside the mainstream activities of each of the military services. Effectively meeting both sets of demands will call for leadership, creativity, and a willingness to challenge traditional institutional priorities. In past times when the nation was confronted with new and grave challenges, its armed forces have always responded with energy and dispatch. There is every reason to believe that they will do so again.